# REALIZE

By

Henry Hoover

For Amanda,

Until next time, my friend.

And for a little community with a big heart in County Tipperary, Ireland.

Stay beautiful.

Dear Reader,

From the bottom of my heart, I hope that you enjoy this book of poetry; volume three in the trilogy: "Three Mysteries/Three Miracles". It is, perhaps, a chronicle of lives being lived; a past that has whirled and winded down a lane to create a life that once could only be dreamed of. I apologize for the fact that there is no table of contents, but what table wants to bear the burden of another's weight day in and day out? Today, we give the table a break. When one takes the courage to wander, he or she is bound to realize; realize personal truths with little "t's" and bits of bigger Truths, as well. We are all bound to realize heartache, joy, the travesty of our Earth/ of our people, and the spirit of love. We are all bound to become ourselves. Read this book from cover to cover, or open it to a random page, but please enjoy the words that have been written and exposed. And please, within the spaces of hollow white, please add pieces of your own soul. Without further ado, I give you Realize.

# Love, Henry

# Dear World

If there is a spot for one to watch

No one specific

Just someone, anyone

For one to watch this world turn 'round

Would it bring upon the one

Previously unimaginable thoughts?

I thought I had been there in a dream

I remember how the Earth

He turned/she turned

Round and round

I wondered when I was there

How it is that continents collide

How it is that people, they collide

Because from where I watched

They were all the same

I wouldn't say "we"

Because I was removed

# Dear World

But, oh, how I remember they were all the same

I return this day and the world

Well, he's the same

She's the same

And I wonder, how I wonder

When will this change?

Equality is fluid

Its form rearranges shape within its container

The most beautiful of which is the human hand

Oh, I beg you, Mother Earth

Oh, I beg you, world in which we live

I cannot continue

I wanted so much

Youth bit me, viper's teeth, youth bit me

Poisoned, I wept

I know not where my feet travel now and then

I know not where my thoughts lead me, here or there

I wanted so much

And memories caress, I beg you Dear World

Please hold us, please hold us

# I Couldn't

I couldn't follow through

Or perhaps even begin

I tried and tried and I'll try again

But often, at sunset,

I perform my retreat

Regress, remember, all tarnished and worn

Shoulders sag, forgiven, forlorn

Morning breaks vertebrae

Bath tub water lines

Line up with life and death

I hold my breath

I always do


Water rushing by, distant, distant

Gold and glitter, I wish if only just to breathe

For a second

For a day

I wish only just to breathe

# I Couldn't

Lungs heaving, tears weaving 'round my face

Stuck in a state, everything bleeds new life into me

New words into me

Currents capture, enrapture, save

Water rushing by

So, I go to sleep

At night

I dream of you, I dream of you

Oh, I fall asleep at night

Shivering from the cold

Water's currents

Running themselves dry

Desert sand once

Laced my vestment

Tucked in, pockets poor

My mouth was full of desert sand

Now water blocks my breath

Flood of heat with sweltering fever, I'm adorned

Ripe, red flood of cold

# I Couldn't

Blue fingers, toes, my body's stunted growth

I remember the fields of cotton glowing white

Calling bright, lit me aglow

Wanted me to sleep in its soft snow

It begged me to lay myself

Down amongst the harvest

It asked me to wrap myself

In its tendrils of white warmth

Desert sands, raging floods

Are silenced in the field

And I lay down

I lie down

I sleep and breathe

Yes, I finally fell asleep

# Drainage Pipes

Understated, pulled too thin to bear

I would have done better, I really would have

Hunched over in a truck, months after

Left me bruised

Do bad things happen to good people?

Or is one naïve to believe anyone is good?

Do these scars burn for a reason?

Does porcelain crack when cold?

All deserve sanctity

A thought I once held dear

Inner sanctum left barren

Open only to those

Who rip, tear, pull

Forlorn shadows pour across smile lines

Calm, caress

## Drainage Pipes

What does it feel like? That golden glow

I see on everyone's face

What does it feel like to grow old?

I once thought I'd die before twenty,

I once thought

I'd never be in that position again

I remember how strong I felt

I had overcome

Maintained my occasional self-worth

Maintained my balance

Or so I thought

They sell themselves, prostitutes

They show themselves to anyone who asks

All because of "he" or "she"

The one who took their good graces away from them

While mine was stolen, I pulled back

Refused to crack


Then, I broke into a million pieces

Shattered and forgave myself for

## Drainage Pipes

Thoughts of it being my fault

For trying to be things I'm not

And strengthened myself


Then he took from me

That monster in the streets

Two months after turning twenty

He took from me what I had reconciled

All the hope I had compiled


For my future, rid of past

Unhindered, upheld and free

But look at me


And he is still out in the streets to hurt

Other unknowing victims


But life is not about caring about such things

People do not care about such things

Do not raise up such things in conversation

# Drainage Pipes

Do not cry while drunk

Do not allow it to pass through your thoughts

This is America

Bathroom floor, I can't stand anymore

Bathroom floor won't hold me any longer

And this surface tension I'm floating on

Seems just about to burst

But I overcame

I won that game

I can't fucking be here, I overcame, I won that game

And never looked back

Loveless, light felt

I kept what scraps of

Myself I felt remained

Refrained from pulling blades

Back and forth

Refrained from pouring toxins forth

## Drainage Pipes

Into my unclenched jaw

Refrained from believing in the slightest of dark thoughts

I hear the drip of dismal drainage pipes

Letting go of all they had previously built up

I want to be like

The drainage pipes

I want to be

Like them

# I Feel Like

A red balloon rises

It rises high and passes the clouds, perhaps

It flies farther than one would

Imagine it could

Tied to its string is a message

"Just love"

What this means, I do not know

But it rises higher than my own spirits can fly

And I watch it rise above my own aspirations

Above my own goals

And I think to myself

This ball of helium and rubber is my own

My own prayer, my own thought

I think to myself

This balloon holds within it

## I Feel Like

All that I cannot scream

All that I cannot

Blast on full

This balloon has the wings

That I wish every day for


I wish every day

To be


Above the

Clouds

# LOSE YOUR

# DIRECTION

# Write/Paint

I remember burning embers slowly smoking from the center

Exhaling only what they had rendered

I paint a picture

The rain becomes the extinguisher

The hiss isn't whispered

Extending the sound that was trapped in clouds

Black overwhelms all the bright lightning showers

As I sat in late hours

Meaning is within the paint

The surfaces, all the same

What it expels, is what you take

And from that it's what you shape

Stay up late, dream all day

Desperate anxiety

Deep found worry

Something says: wait

# Could

It's something hypothetical

Metaphorical but beware

Time, like water, slips

Through fingers open wide

Held aloft gravitating towards

Every new day


There was a time when each war or crime

Could be forgiven, I believed

Long ago, I thought injustice

Would cease

One day


I've got a world

Within my grasp

But I was bitten by a venomous snake

And time takes her toll

I'm stricken, sorrow, thin

## Could

I couldn't linger in a world like that

One without an end of grey days

Delayed, this will take a world of time

Lay down beside rail road tracks

I want to feel the train above me, upon me

I wanted to swell, surrender and drift

I wanted to simply be

You'll find me by those rail road tracks

Cotton fields, sea-shell strewn sea shores

I'm traveling winds, cross-currents

Faded, once gold, glowing

Jaded

Desert sands wisp their ways

About your being

Lay by me

On those rail road tracks

Could

Sure, together we'll go far

And the past she won't bother us

Not no more

Not no more

I gave this world, I gave her hope

Gave him hope

In the morning I woke up

Without a sense of fear

My mirror has since clouded over

Every step I attempt

Is in hesitation of confrontation

Against

A direction unknown

But it was found long ago

To me it was shown

Long ago, with weed or vine

## Could

Overgrown

Now I'm subtle, somber

Somewhere alone

Walking

Along those rail road tracks

Just letting all my time slip past


And if the train never comes

Will I be here waiting?

Will I be here heaving?


Heap upon me your benediction or contradiction

And leave my shoulders light

Suffocation, consecration

Is motivation for a future more pure than the whirlwind

Of whom consumes me, entombs me

More nurturing than the futile devices

Of which surround

# It Is

Family photographs from a time since passed

Boast extravagance

Smiles shine

I don't know where I start or finish

I spent the day

Alone

This will soon diminish

Decompose or fade away

I don't know where

To begin or end

I'll spend the day alone

Again

A feeling of uncertainty

These broken vessels

Will not mend

It Is

I'll start, I'll finish

Concurrently

Lying on my family's trestle

Cut me open

Pull it apart

I thought I saw your

Image

Coming over the horizon

I was uncertain

# FIND YOUR TRUE NORTH

## Objects of Objection

Progression

Underlined words

<u>What are your goals?</u>

Calendars mark

Time lines

Mountain climber's height

Obstacles

Are only those things we see

When we take our eyes

Off of the goal

Sudden remarks

By happenstance

I am over taken

A grocery list

Crumpled, small

A list of things to do

Don't look in the mirror, morning glory

Look at your list crumpled, small

# Crime Is Computing

Crime

It is an atrocious

Crime

The atrophy

Of humanity

Of those

Walking the Earth

A walkway

Vast or infinite

Within the soles

Of our feet

Is it sinister

To be one

Of those who

Bear the silence

## Crime Is Computing

Who witness travesty

With pursed lips

It is sinister

To adhere apathy

To one's soulful vestment

It is horribly

Hurtful

The self-deprecation

Please sing your song on high

It is worrisome

The rate at which we waste away

# BELIEVE

# IN

# YOURSELF

# Embarrassed

Chill mountain air

Collapse

You can see your breath


Pain is waning

Gentle tides

Come and go


Thoughts of there

And then

Could seep

Into your hours


Day break

Progression

Sunlight

Like clock work

Fades towards the future

## Embarrassed

The soon to come

Cold mountain air

Hold your breath

Everyone does the same routine

Everyone follows the footfalls

You can see your breath

As you ask yourself

Where am I?

Where have I been?

What are we doing with our time left on Earth?

And just where

Am I going?

# Decisions

Alone

Slow moving river

Rocks worn smooth

By currents centuries old

Sharing birthdays with red woods

Or fossilized oak

Sadness lingers

Fall leaves caught in the currents

Catch a moment alone

You'll never feel like one

Until you're alone

# Say

A direction to go

Sometimes I feel

I'm flying

I miss those words these days

Follow through just follow through

I tell myself at night

Follow through

Just follow through

Protected by the cold


Say

You worry from time to time

Or send your thoughts my way

Honestly

I fear for this

I'm tangled

When I reminisce

Thorns have grown in

  Say

           Once pleasant gardens, groves

                I walked barefoot

                Bloody and scarred

                Sometimes I feel

                      Lost


                       Still


                 I harbor the ability

                To conceive a direction

                       To go

                 I hold the momentum

                       To go

# Gain Control

Oh, and to be out of control

Well

There certainly was never a sort of thing

Oh, and to bear

Vestments of gold

Or brass

Rosaries hang

Are held

In Mass


To ruin a day

Or three or four

Lifeless, left squandered

On the bathroom

Floor


"Out of control"

Well, There

## Gain Control

Is no such thing

Until being

Begets remembrance

But to be far

From control

Well, that's just choice

Take it with

A pillar of salt

# Be

Anger glory, red

Not for the lack of action

From any one of them

All of them

More for something summer felt

I read sipping tea


More for someone

Summer long

You gnaw, gnash away


I'm bearing more

Broken, sore

Blisters, calloused eyes


Shed tears and you're angry

Not for personal lack of action

I'm angry for personal obstruction

  Be


        Where were you

        Who are you

        Where are we

        And where does it

        Hurt


        I felt throughout

        Rigid pain

        Everyday

        Where do I go from here

        What is most important


        Hands descend

        They fall

        Their place as stepping stones

        Help me win the race


        On a cliff, I stood

        I stand

# Be

Beneath me fields of green

Summer whisper

Faint heart beat

Mountain's thunder deep

A summer only dreamed

Sun high, favor warmth

One summer wrote this

Rebuilt, metamorphoses

One cannot be rebuilt if

Destroyed, no token

Of human affection

It is better to grow than to remain broken

## Wet Lakes

Reflections ripple

Cause trifle

Glorious deep

Cold casts

The first stone

Land or pier

Water pulls

Towards shore

Your feet, below

Sweet glint, light ablaze

Together

We are pulled

Into its depths

This wet

Lake

# O World, O Japan

Earth we feel

I shake, we shudder

Earth we hear your harm

Our presence, our nature

Retaliation is your gun

In my gut I fall, I foil

I'm lying on your grounds

My ears are pressed upon you

Your grounds misery latent

Erupts

Across continents

Borders, waves

Passed lines drawn by man


We scream

Like you

We scream for help like you

And now

## O World, O Japan

O World

O, I scream, I shudder

Nuclear waste pours from my mouth, my face

And now O World, I beg, I apologize

For all of my brothers, my sisters

Their haste in bringing you harm

And secretly we're kindred

It's not far off at all

I'm alone in this world

And so are you

They scramble to bring pain to one another

Pausing only when your belly quakes

I'm left alone

O Earth

And I need you

How I need you

To hold me

## O World, O Japan

Come hold me

I feel your heart aflame

O World

I press my ear against your

Grounds

I'll promise

We'll find a Way

But until that time

That day does

Shine

Please don't

Leave me alone

# Acupuncture

Needles and numbers

Pins adhered

To flesh

An overdeveloped

Pin cushion

Or stress ball

If you

Are "into

That kind of thing"

Maps

My skin

Both hold needles

Well

Or so I was

Told 4 years

3 months

Had blood of gold

## Acupuncture

With scorched, red

Earth

Palms and feet

A binary star

With a particular

Taste for

Acupuncture

Galaxies

Space dust

Or cosmic clouds

Harbor anything

But pins and needles

## Come Back

Come back

And come back I say again

Twice no three times over

Until soft, gently whispered

It'll return

For I speak not of you

Or you

Or you

But of that one hiding from

Once thought in

But hiding from

The hall of mirrors

Treachery or misery

Or everything in between

Everything now

## Come Back

And then

Filling forms

Stars and blank white sheets

Solemn thoughts precede desire

Or actions best placed on hold

I'll hold my tongue

My neck and noose

Once you come again


The hall of mirrors

Burn, terror

Torture

Young and frail

I thought of myself

I looked at myself


And saw

Nothing at all

I realized

Then

## Come Back

My canvas is blank and white

Like sheets

I'll paint

Those mirrors


Away

Or over

Their disarray

And wear my disillusionment well

YOUR

LIFE IS

MADE OF

LIGHT

# Mourning Wars and Kites

I forgot how to walk

To and fro

I saw waves carry bridal showers

On Eastern shores

Cloudy water filled only those

Vessels with opacity

Or structural invisibility

When spring or dawn

Came to be,

Green grass meets concrete

Asphalt forms walls, boundaries

Dream or designate

Delusions preoccupy

Letting go

Picture hands letting go

Of all they carry/hold

# Mourning Wars and Kites

Lungs are moist,

Warm and thick

Expansion

But often

Contraction;

Watching idly by

As minute-hands strike 9's

Thoughts inhibit

But compasses can break

Moss grows in search

Of the Northern Star

And lands of ice and chill

I want to be welcomed,

I hope for all but pain

If kind adulation

Goes unheard

If your ears or mine

Are caked with leaves and grime,

Then perhaps

The forest

## Mourning Wars and Kites

Will welcome us soon

But I'm hoping

If only,

And yearning

If only,

And forgetting English in grace

Failing form or feathers

Plucked one

By one

Tie your tongue in knots

A kiss

Electricity or fire

Water nourishes

Earth and sky

Covers all

Mourning wars,

Embraces all

Kites

# If Giving Up Means Finding an End

End me/unwind me

My maker, note-taker;

Shield my failing form

I'm too tired,

Beaten, heavy

To be sheltered from the storm

Broken, worn

And falling hard

I want rebirth, to be reborn

But palpitating hearts

Are still beating

And my tears flow freely when I cry

So moisture clings upon my lips

Telling me to try

Time still hovers

Over water clean as spring

And my reflection's ripple is granting

## If Giving Up Means Finding An End

Hindsight

"I can't continue"

I hear at night

Every day is a new battle fought

What's real today, what direction

Is not your way

But mine?


What steps must I take to learn

From my bruises, or

Untie the noose around my neck

Tied tightly around my neck

A weighted catch

I'm caught and captured

I will resist

I will persist

I will not detract and desist


I am vulnerable

Therefore, I exist

# A Hope

I guess I give up

Where did I find,

No, where did they,

(On my heart,

On my ribs)

Where did these,

(On my back,

Down my legs)

Where did the

Cracks begin?

Where did these ruptures start?

Focus on grey,

I focused on the sky

Heavy spirits, shoulders remain

Scarred

Disgust in the world, further,

In myself

## A Hope

Save your visible aura

Of gold, shining forgiveness

Myself, I'm disgusted

In the world, in myself,

I'm disgusted

Save for your kind eyes' vision,

For ages or eons we suffer

Our suffering

We suffer the stench of our vain airs, I suffer

Every day I

Lose my way towards you

Or every day

I feel your lighthouse beacon bright

Has dimmed within my eyes

This is no fault of yours

But mine

My eyes are throbbing

Destitute of tears

They are retribution

# A Hope

I fear, I'm naked

Shaking, scared

I hurt to stand for those who

Spear; I struggle

Safety, come at last

Place that smile on my face

And bring to me a new

Day of direction

To you


And I'm a fool,

I know this truth

I know how perfect things once were

And now I feel

Change and now

I see a change

In you and I

And I beg you,

Don't fall

## A Hope

Because you're my light and

You're my wind

Beneath my wings

And you make me smile, always

And do not fall,

Because I never told you just how

Brave, just how

Beautiful you really are

I've always thought you deserve

A world devoid of rust

PAIN

IS NOT

PERMANENT

# I Like My Name, I Never Said That

The art of words and colors

The art of in-between

I've given up my search

Based on what I've seen

I spoke words of hate

My day of birth

While the moon was high

It was out of sadness

Acid rain and cheap, cheap wine

I dreamed of storms


They shimmer

I dream of saints

And a seraph

I want to paint love and truth

I want to speak it

More, I want to have it

## I Like My Name, I Never Said That

Most of all

He called me once

An angel, I thought

"Look in the mirror."

I never did say it


I never quite could

All I did was

The opposite

Of the raging rivers inside

## Here's To Icebergs

Practice simple

Multiplication;

Instant gratification,

Euphoric states

And river beds

Will release their

Sunken treasures upon

Our barren chests


I never understood

What it meant

To be first born

But I know a heart-broken rib cage

All too well and that

The sea shore's second tide

Brings waves of fury and

Brightly shed sorrow tears

## Here's To Icebergs

What isn't worth electric apathy?

Wings are used

To fly but also forget

The morning dove never met

The dawn singing this

Sad song; it is truth

All the same


Icebergs expose

Only a fraction of

Their being and

From them I learned

So well; it is

Worth the risk

To sink sailing ships

If only to keep the water from boiling


Green grass summers

And Christmas trees

Keep my heart at bay

## Here's To Icebergs

But I don't know how

To bear my love

Without forgetting

How to listen

And I pay the price

For this painful recognition

By bleaching my spirit free

It seems every time

My heart is hurt

I run further and

Further away

## Swimming with Sharks

I found myself

Beach beneath

My heavy thoughts

And sun-dried sighs

The water beckoned

Only at sunset

The water called

When the stars and the moon

Made their appearances, golden

And soft

Wading, unfurling

Toes in moist sand

Waves pushing me back

Then pulling me

Forward

I found myself

## Swimming with Sharks

Neutral buoyancy

Neutral states

Body beneath surface tension

Liquid embrace

Currents enact

Their core desire

And sharks hear me

Creep into the sea


I thought I heard dolphin songs

And a whale's whisper

But the sharks

They hear me creep into the sea


Still, I found myself

When sharks

They swam, swarmed about

And above the water

The bees didn't sting, they knew I

Was a flower

## Swimming with Sharks

But I am not their own

And the sharks, they're beasts

I thought I knew

Better than to bleed

In their presence

It was then that

I found myself when

The bees left me

Alone, I'm not theirs

Beneath the water

In the sky

I am a flower

The sharks tasted

Pollen, not knowing

It was my blood

I breathed in

Only water

## Swimming with Sharks

Before only venom

Like sharp scorpion bite

And realized

The bees did not conquer

The sharks did not feed

I was protected

Though I thought

I was the most

Vulnerable

I had ever been

## The Forests

There are forests

We knew them well

Perhaps never forgot

Their whispering winds

Songs and dry spells

Rain, storms and lightning

Their bows bend beneath

Heaps of snow

And winters' chill


They call to me

And I forgot

Or placed far behind

A place

The place where I

Forgot how to be happy

I never forgot the trees

I just forgot how

## The Forests

To be

Happy


Now they call me

Once again

We knew them well,

The forests

They call my name

And I tell them


I

Am hurrying,

I'm hurrying

The world

One day shall

Rest


We knew them well

The forests

## The Forests

The evergreens and elms

I imagine a forest

Of Christmas trees

And I smile

The lights lit up

The colors

Lit up

All the colors of

The rainbow

And yellow golden white

Russian winters

And Oregon trails

I don't know

How I forgot

# Tornadoes Tear Through

Disheveled in disdain

There's nothing

More that

Could remain

And love is nothing

With price or pair

Love is free

Or so I thought

It should be given

Brought, but

Tides bring in words

Written in sea foam

All that I had

Given, they gave

## Tornadoes Tear Through

Asp's poison and

A viper's strike

And only ask

For more

And in the past

Years since gone

I've learned these lessons


Lessons

How I've learned

These lessons

But know from whence

I came

And mirrors show me

Memories behold

How the camel's back

Can only hold so much

And a person's virtue

Is simply so

## Tornadoes Tear Through

Though it may not

Be wisdom, wise


An independent vessel

Says I am my own

I distribute keys upon

My discretion, alone


And there are those

Who, with force,

Tried to pry open rusting

Locks

But my words


They belong

To my tongue


They are shared

With whom I please

And my seasons

## Tornadoes Tear Through

Brought, seasons

Bring climate change

And colored leaves

So summer winds

Run rivers route

Surging waters

Take me away

And freedom's bells

Ring in my heart

Showing me the way

And night terrors

Are left behind along

With hollow egos

# I Don't Give

I don't give a fuck

Crude, I know

But every morning

I wake up

A reminder

Is necessary,

What day is this?

Oh, it is

The ninth

Or the tenth

Or so on,

And so forth

When days

They begin to tumble

I cannot believe my eyes

Do they deceive

Me or receive me

## I Don't Give

Do I even have control?

I dreamed once of smiling

Beyond my own control

I dreamed once of

Flying over borders

Man made.

Where art thou,

Where are you?

The one

To set me free

Set me from my

Despondency

Save me

From my

Tragedy, she is an

Ill omen

Hollow at her best

# I Don't Give

I don't know where

It is I'm going

But, day to day,

I will try

Water flows

Rapid current set

And when my eyes ponder upon

Just what it is

They see

Bamboo shoots

And bamboo leaves

They fill my vision, free

I call upon

This despondency

To hold me in

The night

I call upon

Apathy

## I Don't Give

To show me

I'm not right

But when

Day to day

All remains the same

I know

I need change


I thought I could

I thought I would

Bring it upon myself;

And the thing I wonder, I yearn,

I want

You


I need you


I am a bird

Your sky,

A place I want to be

## I Don't Give

And certainly

The Lord,

He watches

Over me


But who is He?


Watching over me


Who is He?

# Movements

And movements

They take us forward

Your divorce or his divide

These movements,

They drive us


Till dawn

I couldn't tell you

This from that

But movements

They fill my mind


Children, pets, rent on time

Forward somersault

Draw a bath

Slip, dip, drip

Birthday cakes

Epiphanies

## Movements

Remember when

You were young?

When will

Everything

Change


Movements move

Us forward through

Newly formed

Wrinkles

New every day


If two months

Prior

From this exact moment

You felt a certain way

You certainly defined

Your past

And your future

You prayed

## Movements

Head bowed

Eyes close

Contrite

But surroundings

Altered

By happenstance

It's not the same

It's not the same

There's a wall

Behind us

It's been pushin'

Since birth

It will not stop until our demise

Fall down

It moves forward

Try to go back

It moves us forward

## Movements

Just run ahead

Run ahead

Motions move us forward

Any given day

I will be different

In a week

I will be different

In a month

In a year

Instantaneously

Motion is growth

## I Couldn't Understand

Time delays

Bullet points

Form rhythmically

A mental form

For daily motion

Reuse, refuse, repeat

I can't push farther

Than my own feet

Are willing to go

Or my will

Coils

More over

Makes my tongue

Swollen

Cold

Turn the clock

## I Couldn't Understand

Days ahead

Reuse, refuse, repeat


If thoughts of you

Did glitter gold

Oh how much time


I'd have


If thoughts of another

Held stories told

But where would

I find

The time?

# Of Course

You ever shiver

Too cold to get out of bed?

You ever shiver

After being touched

Shedding your clothes

For someone long dead

Who promised you

Gold, got misery instead?

You ever shiver

Twist and turn

After you looked

In the mirror

Only bloody abrasions

Won't heal

You ever shiver

When you think

## Of Course

How you're not

Strong enough for today

And tomorrow's still comin'

You ever feel

Morning tides pull


Close your eyes for a second

Morning tides pull

You ever feel suffocation

And breathing won't help

Because the fist

Around your throat

Is metaphorical, though real

Ever read a poem

'Bout a girl

Beaten and raped

In Ethiopia


Did it make you feel ill?

## Of Course

Or did you breeze on by

A reality thousands of

Miles away

Unjustified

Surreal


Beaten and raped

In Ethiopia

Beaten and raped in Europe

Beaten and raped in America

Ever been raped


Ever been beaten

Ever been beaten and raped

And written a poem?


Did it make you feel attractive?

Did it make you feel whole?

Did it make you feel wanted?

Did the pity ease your wounds

## Of Course

Or is it time that heals?

Fall into a maelstrom

Only bloody abrasions


Forget your past

They'll never understand

Oh, you can talk

About it

Oh, you can weep about it

But fucking grow up

At least you aren't in Syria

# Something More

Airplane, aisle side

Skip a beat

Hearts starts

Skipping beats

Window seat

Be more appropriate

Will be more beautiful

Move towards it

Nausea lost

Its hold

Worlds since past

Breathe easy

Currents spread

## Something More

Oceans wide

Breaking waves

For more to come


Holistic healing

Self-taught art

Bend light with

Your eyes

Vision


Malleable


Air and sea

Are true for thee

Though

Land held under

Never loved another

More


Than your foot steps

## Something More

Gently pressed

In soil, moist

All together


You don't have wings

The Earth and sea

Are home for me

Sky's only

The place to be


When

Airplane, aisle side

Setting all

In motion

Spin.

# I Don't Know Who Means To Hurt Me

My mind held

By moon swept

Rhymes and solar

Rays of disarray

Say take control of

All I have

Inside, on shoulder

Tough and sweet

Under callous, you'll

Find bone

But deeper still

You'll find home

Something I lost

Long ago

I don't know

Who means to

## I Don't Know Who Means To Hurt Me

Hurt me, at times

It is so unclear

I fear all those

Around me, save for

The cats, the dogs the dear

The birds

Whisper to skies

Above, the wolves

Speak to the ground

And I stand

On both

I stand on riverbeds

These growing pains

Are lightning bolts

In the clouds

NOW TAKE
A LOOK
AROUND
YOU

# WHAT DO YOU SEE

# No Matter

The rain falls

Different types of light

Caught up in drops

The wind's direction

Is all on its own

Home does not exist

No matter how far north

No matter how far south

Home exists in the heart


Treasure, green, millions

Of individuals -

Are snowflakes and blades of grass really all the same?

I try to count each one

They are all their own entities

They are all, each exactly the same

# No Matter

The summer has passed

But I am the fall

The following burst of fresh, the morning's shiver crawling

Down your spine

I forgot who I am

Days of the week

And minute hands

Momentary loss

Eternal gain and

Will this feeling remain?

The lives of those all in their

Rooms, the rain falls

Different types of light caught up in drops

Flashes across their faces

We are all in this together

# No Matter

This race towards the finish line

This time spent in the waiting line

Warm water across your face

And what will tomorrow bring


We made mistakes

We made the most out of

The miracles, our hearts do not

Stop beating until the day we die


When I look

At your face, it's never the same

The more we learn the less we know

## Ocean's Floor

Many things drift across my heart and eyes

Many things and I let them

Collect like barnacles and brine

And lead weights shaped like upside-down balloons

They pull me underwater

Without granting me the opportunity

To breathe or speak, so I sink

Deeper still, until the ocean's floor

Is the only place I see

All of which is ok, if I don't struggle

When I finally learn to accept those

Certain truths that forced me under

In the first place, and an entirely

Different world lives before my eyes

I'd cry or shed a tear if it wouldn't just blend in

## Ocean's Floor

Against the sea's salt water canvas

I am pulled with the current

And thankfully so

Because without that force

I would have nowhere else to go

But I am not dead; I can feel it in my body

In my veins, my heart creates little ripples

My soundless words, little bubbles

The fish and eels surround without a sound

The orcas and baleen whales linger

Whispering tales of times to come

And those since passed

So I watch the world flow by

All the tiny neon lights, glowing fish drifting by

And my friend the moon never looked so beautiful

Above the waves broken light,

A cascade of moments in time

I know that it will help me, low tide, by my side

## Ocean's Floor

The moon will set me free

I try to swim but nothing else

Can pull me from my seat in the soil

At the bottom of the ocean, it's floor

Means more to me

Than all of those things

I could never

And won't

Know

# Spatial Rhythm

Everything makes sense

Or my senses are

Engulfed in serendipity

And fruitful labor

Torn between virtues

Torn across continents

And life flows deeply

Out at sea or safe at bay

Whispering words across

Stars and wind

Fireflies' convalescence

Never held more nostalgia

Planetary pull, gravity

Bears different weight

Takes you down

Harder, faster, depending

## Spatial Rhythm

Where you are

In regards to the sun

I feel a fool once more

A feeling I can't explain

Or describe

English holds limits

Of its own like

International borders

Being familiar yet foreign

But I feel a

Fool once more for

Years of painstaking

Heart breaking misery

I've put upon myself

An internal mystery

I've realized was

## Spatial Rhythm

All my own

Creation; by

Creation I mean

I had the power

All along to lead

My feet in stride

With a gravitational rhythm

From each planet

To the sun

A solar system

Is a collection

Of unified processes

And patterns

Replicated on Earth

And within us

Our cells know this

All too well

# To You, Two Spirit

Freedom rings

Through words of Kant

All that one can

Do and should

One must not hurt

Another, take advantage

Of another or his/her

Ourselves, This and that

Are possible but it's

What must be done

I'm thankful our

Children have clean

Water to drink down

Where the rivers run

And if our cups

Hold fluoride no

## To You, Two Spirit

Paste within those

Liquid tears, I'm

Thankful all the

Same, the water's

Nearly pure

Descartes said our

Senses rule

Sans an iron fist

Berkley, our perception

Is so much more than

This, I hear the water

Running, she washes

Another dish, my hands

Swing and sway to offer

Aid, but perhaps it's not

My place, in my heart

## To You, Two Spirit

However, "beneath the heavens

With awe", though different,

Peculiar, strange, I

Harbor within me

My own mortal law


They cut off Olympe's

Head and threw it on

The ground, her body

Lay limp and dead

Her soul, forever on

Women stand tall

Your heads up strong

The race is nearly

Won

And those of

You two-spirited true

Fear not the rule of "right"

## To You, Two Spirit

For it is inherent within

Each other to live on Earth

As one

For what place

Must man take

And women where

Is yours?

It is within our

Own choosing, neither

Above nor below

There are those

Their veins are

Blue, deep within

Hides red, virginal

Venus and Apollo's

Postulate, ambiguous

Words lay dormant

## To You, Two Spirit

Potential energy at

Its best, don't

Fret or worry

Is disdain in

Search of shoes

To fill, we are

Our own cobblers, seamstresses, and sage

We are our own industrial revolution

Our very own steel mill

## Key Holes

Key holes

And fancy, darling things

Hanging from a ring

Six keys

All hanging in a row

Tumbling tides once took us

Mountain ranges sung

And birds spoke of

Rose petals, fungus

And Christmas time fun

Candles led the way

By night, stars were our

Bodhisattvas


Key holes

## Key Holes

Now litter my chest

And within my universe

Galaxies threaten to collide

In stride

With all that is pulling us

Forward

Towards a future far too distant

To see

The sun on my chin

A glowing mystery, a memory

Of time spent in shady groves

A chocolate colored tree

Its bark begs us to listen

Our necks speak truths

Of Mother Earth and feathers

Grace our cheeks

Still, cupid's arrows struck me

Still, I quietly bleed

## Key Holes

Tears fall from my face

And a breeze carries them still

All the piercings I've never gotten

Are constant reminders of all of those times

I didn't need to feel pain

Eyes stare at Saint Sebastian's despair

He's honest and true, you know

But for all the time

Spent beneath the microscope

His tattoos speak tales of gold

Screaming and singing

"There's always time to grow".

And cupid strikes again

He mended the coffee cup

That plagued my dreams for a year

# Mother America

A woman is more than these three things

A womb, some breasts, and a diamond ring

Time, a moving wall

It pushes us, detests us, dares us all

And gravity pulls us down


A birthday party

Mother America bought me a cake

I'm 11 today, but I can't

Really remember

She said that I could draw

Whales like they were real

And the morning casts light on us

I think I remember now

Rainy days, she spent inside

I picked her all of the desert flowers

## Mother America

In the mud, outside

Every now and then

I would say something

And she would smile

As if to say

"Now, in this moment,

All that I do for you is worth it"

The moon cascades her in brilliance, fatigue

I cry from time to time

In the night

While she hides the hours

That have passed us by

Her halo is made of

All those nights

Praying for my safety

# The Dance

Venus and Jupiter danced

They said everything would be ok

Behind wreaths of garland

Filled with gifts

1, 1, 2, 3, 5, 8, 13, 21, 34

Pine cones, mistletoe

And things we bear

Upon backs

Bent over under the weight from it all

Day to night

Day to night

We boil and blister

Swim and remember

All the time since passed

Bullet holes, my blazon

You were like a gun

## The Dance

But autumn leaves

Fill the holes

Fill my voids

In gentle surrender

To their magnificence

Spring blooms in me

Continuously, coupled

With winter's chill

But all the sweat

That has dripped from my pores

Tells me infinity is as easy as 1,2,3

Building blocks of creativity

But even oblong shapes and love

Won't protect me from the tears

So, I have become a jellyfish

# The Dance

Of "the vine"

My only wish is that

I was dead

Dead to the stinging sensation

I leave behind

And bubbles float above the space

Where I struggle to hold my breath


I sit on a shell, behind a book

You wrote it

I think

A story of my life

But it was never really mine

Bits and pieces blare truth,

And tumble with the rest

Until I open my eyes


There's a lamb behind me

## The Dance

And a book beside me

There's a lamb behind me

And a book inside me

I cut open my stomach once

I held guts before the world

I realized I held shame


It was never really mine to hold

Only words they used grown old

Thrown at me

To break me, hurt me

Straddle, hold

Until I'd quit it, dismiss it

And be just like them

But Christmas trees

Shimmer and speak

Telling me

Remember only the words of love

# Grow

Astral planes of existence

Coupled with my foolish persistence

I was a pillar of doubt.

My disbelief, a sudden relief

When I discovered the rising sun

Come undone and fall from mountain tops to the far between

It's profound, unbound, faster than the speed of sound

Is my soul flying?

This soil, moist and fertile,

"Oh, the things that you will grow"

Our words are whispered when stories are told

I hear the horizon ringing clear

Nameless and many are the rivers running into the sea

They are the feelings pulsing from beneath my skin

When I discovered the sun

. For rays of light do not withhold life from anything or anyone.

No, rays of light do not withhold life.

## Grow

I feel the eons passing us by.

I am fixated by the miracle of light.

I was a pillar of salt.

And it's not from a lack of luster

That they choose not to speak

In the rustling of leaves noisily down the streets

Against black concrete:

The virtue of leaves and flower petals, too.

The virtue of their burden; green, pink, blue color hue

They say to the bees, "It's all for you."

Roots in the ground, roots in the sky, delicate

But so precious to behold from one's eyes

Their sentience, the trees, their radiance, the flowers

Listen in the forests, listen in the fields.

It's not from a lack of luster that they choose not to speak.

Steadily they climb, steadily they grow.

And I want to be like them

Photosynthesis, and in parenthesis,

(just another way to breathe)

The plants are all that we know that by their life

# Grow

They keep us alive.

Curb side and straining,

The grass manages to grow while a chill wind blows,

I can hear the leaves rustling,

It sounds the same in any language.

The chloroplast gave emerald its name

And our lungs a fighting chance,

Something we rarely give ourselves.

And I remember: you told me

The vines grow to produce fruit.

You told me the vines, they grow for us.

You told me it's the simple things;

The shade beneath a tree, the color of autumn

You told me the forests are our friend and they will win.

I felt small, today.

Walking on the Earth, a speck on the Earth

The soil cold and moist, I felt small

Knowing I could plant a seed and it would grow.

I felt tall knowing, I reap what I sow, and the like the grass, curb side and reaching, we're trying

# Realize

As days drift by

Or seem to pause

Everything stands still

Save glints of dust in light

Years filed away

In my mind

Blow in the breeze

You created

Or perhaps it was me

And I feel

I am a fool

I know

I am the fool

How do you tell your mother

Tell your father

The only reason

You sigh sometimes

## Realize

Is because you watched

The news

How to do explain

To family, friends

You want

It to end

To leave you alone

Are you

Supposed to apologize


Maybe I am

Maybe that is all it takes

How to explain

To people on the street

You only want to

Be treated

As you treat others

I only try to give

Love and all I have

I only want to love

## Realize

And I go to sleep at night

Alone every night

I fell in love

Too long ago

It wasn't love

But faux admiration

I fell in love

Not too long ago

It is real

Heavy, hard

Further still

He makes me happy

Happy

Happy

I saw him

Just the other day

I fell asleep

My soul soaring

How do you tell someone that?

I've realized

## Realize

I need to stop

Insulting myself

In the mirror

I think everyone

Is so beautiful

And so handsome

But never me

Everyone is so smart

And so talented

But never me

I need to tell myself

I am beautiful, handsome

Smart and talented

Because they're

Living their own lives

As I walk down

Fog drenched

Leaf laden streets

How do I tell him

He's so brave

## Realize

He deserves gold and stars

And bumble-bee

Flower farms, Christmas trees

And honey comb

Maybe

First

I need to tell myself

I deserve the same

My brothers

My older and younger

How I love them so

I want to smile for them

Always

And my parents how I love

Them so

I want to make them proud

And my friends

My heart skips beats

When I hear them laugh

I want them to be happy

## Realize

I want the world to be happy

But how can I want this

When I don't know how to be

The same

To be

Further, still

To stay happy


Imagine

If the United Nations

Existed to plan surprise parties

For all the other countries

Imagine

If America was not at war

Afghanistan, Iraq

Imagine if we gave

Gifts instead of bombs

Imagine if Pakistan, Syria

And India

If Muslims and Christians

### Realize

And Jews

Black, brown, or white

What if we didn't fight

But had love wars

Who could be nicer to the others

Always?

What if people traveled to

Chechnya

To attend their annual bake sale?

Would we all wake up one day

Realize we're all the same?

What if we all shared our food

What if we all adopted

Never left a child

Without a home

Imagine if two people

Who were in love

And it was real and it was right

If they were two males

Or females

## Realize

Imagine if they could get

Betrothed

Anywhere

Any time

And it wasn't a big deal

How do I tell

My friends, family

Him

That is all I want

That maybe

When this day comes

I will be happy

Because love makes me a fool

Oh, yes

It makes me a fool

But when this day comes

We will all be fools

Perhaps that is the meaning

Of life

I heard

## Realize

That charity feels

Like heroin

Why can't it be our heroin?

Why can't we all be fools?

I believe the world wants to

We all want to

Be fools in love

With each other

With Mother

Father

Earth

We all are fools in love


No one has ever made me want to better myself

Truly

Be better, truly

See the world

Fully

I am his fool

Everyone's fool

You

Are

Everything

# Visions

Alleviation comes in moments

Abound and a cloud

A wave

Covers me

A tapestry

Of blue and old

Thoughts since passed


How much longer

Could we live like this

Contend with this

Eternal bliss

Is not ignorance


How much longer

[133]

Visions

Will the window pane

Hold our attention

Dirty glass

But past it, beauty

When summer has long since

Gone, your streets are filled

With winter's fog

Lamps aglow

Allow us to know

You're still smooth,

Alive

Oh, how much longer

Will motions turn

A vision's brief life

## Visions

Holds, for me, an

Eternity

But this cannot last

This uncertainty


I crave freedom, or

Do I fear it? I crave his touch

Or your embrace,

No, I miss it


I yearn to drink

From liberty's streams

Yet, bathe in them nightly

Beneath lunar songs

Taking it for granted,

All felt wrong, disgusting

Pathetic

# Visions

But love is a vessel now suited

For my broken form

Life is a lover who caresses and soothes

Oh, how much longer

Until all goes full circle

Until three hundred or sixty

Plus more, comes to fruition

I thirst for my childhood ambition, Intention

Inability to listen

Hands over ears, my life is my own

My future is my own

Or I have only grown

And will not allow you to become a stumbling block

For my narrow path


Narrow only at times brief moments

Which, for me,

Hold an eternity

www.ingramcontent.com/pod-product-compliance
Lightning Source LLC
Chambersburg PA
CBHW031400040426
42444CB00005B/366